USBORNE

FIRST BOOK OF
BRITAIN

Sophy Tahta

Illustrated by Colin King
Designed by John Barker

Contents

2	About Britain		18	The North West
4	The story of Britain		20	The North East
6	London		22	Wales
8	The West Country		24	Southern Scotland
10	The South Coast		26	Central Scotland
12	The heart of England		28	Northern Scotland
14	East Anglia		30	Northern Ireland
16	The Midlands		32	Index

About Britain

Britain is the largest island in Europe. It is made up of three countries: England, Scotland and Wales. Britain and Northern Ireland form the United Kingdom (UK), which is shown here. Each country is divided into smaller areas called counties or regions. These are shown in detail later in the book.

The Union Jack

The Union Flag of the UK is known as the Union Jack. It is made up of the English, Irish and Scottish flags which are named after the patron saints of these countries. The Welsh flag is also shown here.

St George's Cross of England.

St Patrick's Cross of Ireland.

St Andrew's Cross of Scotland.

The Red Dragon of Wales.

Language

The Irish, Scottish and Welsh languages were first spoken by people called the Celts over 2000 year ago. They are still spoken in these countries today along with English, and are used on road signs.

CARDIFF
CAERDYDD

Weather

The UK has mild, changeable weather and quite a lot of rain which makes its countryside green and lush. The west coast is warmed by an ocean current called the Gulf Stream.

WESTERN ISLES

SKYE

NORTHERN IRELAND

Belfast

EIRE

This part of Ireland is called the Republic of Eire. It is not part of the UK.

ATLANTIC OCEAN

ISLES OF SCILLY

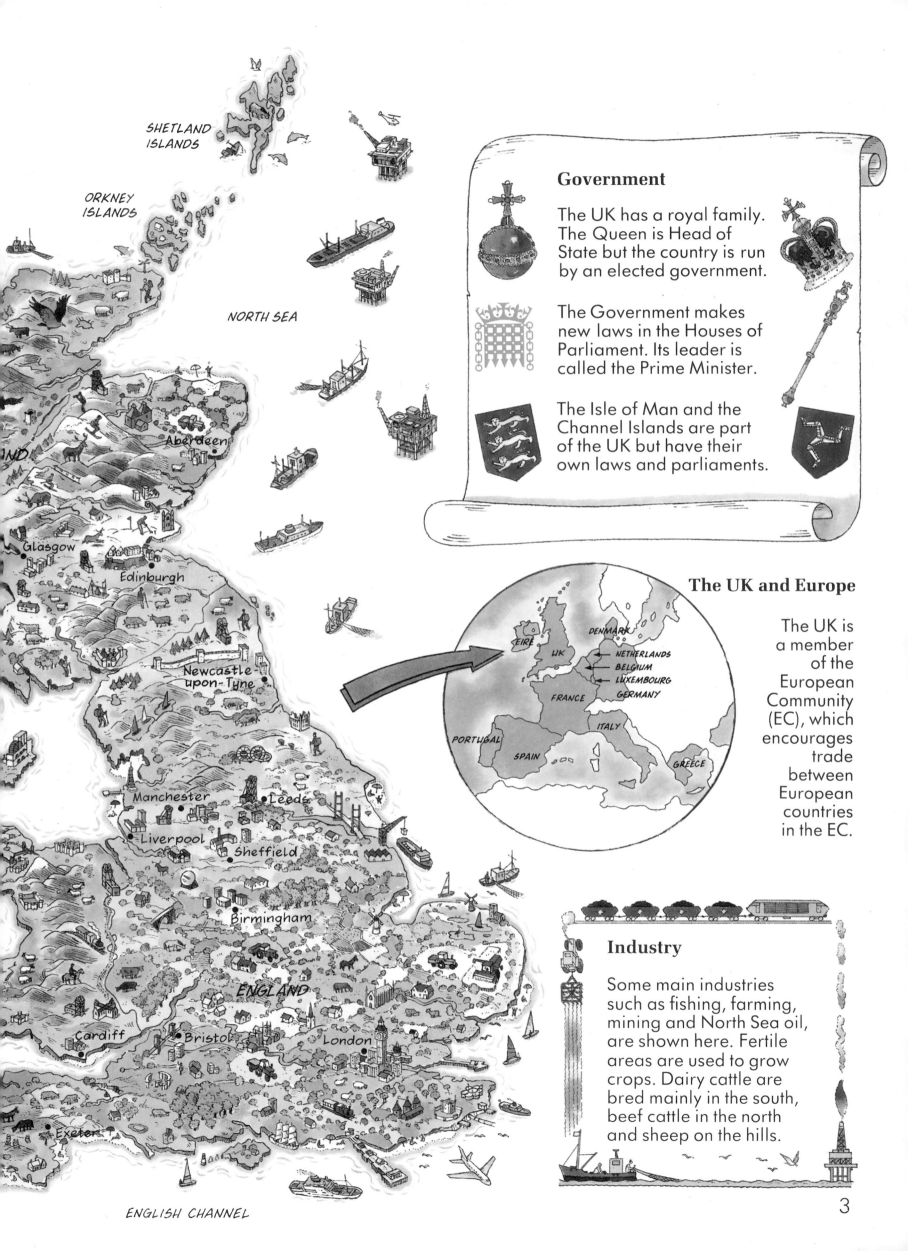

SHETLAND ISLANDS

ORKNEY ISLANDS

NORTH SEA

Aberdeen

Glasgow

Edinburgh

Newcastle-upon-Tyne

Manchester

Liverpool

Leeds

Sheffield

Birmingham

ENGLAND

Cardiff

Bristol

London

Exeter

ENGLISH CHANNEL

Government

The UK has a royal family. The Queen is Head of State but the country is run by an elected government.

The Government makes new laws in the Houses of Parliament. Its leader is called the Prime Minister.

The Isle of Man and the Channel Islands are part of the UK but have their own laws and parliaments.

The UK and Europe

EIRE

UK

DENMARK

NETHERLANDS

BELGIUM

LUXEMBOURG

GERMANY

FRANCE

ITALY

PORTUGAL

SPAIN

GREECE

The UK is a member of the European Community (EC), which encourages trade between European countries in the EC.

Industry

Some main industries such as fishing, farming, mining and North Sea oil, are shown here. Fertile areas are used to grow crops. Dairy cattle are bred mainly in the south, beef cattle in the north and sheep on the hills.

The story of Britain

THE STONE AGE
About 15000 – 2100 BC (Before Christ)

THE BRONZE AGE
About 2100 – 700 BC

THE IRON AGE
About 700 BC – 43 AD (Anno Domini)

The first people in Britain lived in caves and gathered plants and hunted wild animals, thousands of years ago. This time is called the Stone Age after the stone tools and weapons they used.

During the late Stone Age (or Neolithic Age) groups of people arrived here from Europe. They settled in villages and farmed. In the Bronze Age they learned how to make tools from bronze.

Iron Age Britain was ruled by warlike Celtic tribes from Europe. The Celts made things from bronze and iron and decorated them with lovely swirling designs. They later became known as the Britons.

THE MIDDLE AGES
1066 — 1485

Britain was then conquered by Normans from northern France who built strong stone castles and cathedrals. Their duke, William, became king when he beat the Saxons near Hastings in 1066.

The next 400 years are called the Middle Ages. The Normans were followed by kings from the royal families of Plantagenet, Lancaster and York, who fought endless battles here and abroad.

During this time, a plague called the Black Death killed thousands of people; mighty barons set up the first parliament to advise the king and angry peasants revolted against harsh laws and unfair taxes

THE STUARTS
1603 — 1714

THE GEORGIAN AGE
1714 — 1837

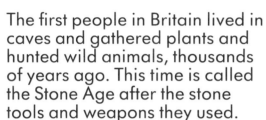

The early Stuarts quarrelled with Parliament. This led to civil war in 1642. Parliament won and Oliver Cromwell ruled as Lord Protector. The kings and queens who ruled later had less and less power.

The Georgian Age is named after several kings called George who followed the Stuarts. During this time, people left to begin new lives abroad and Britain fought the French Emperor, Napoleon.

The Agricultural and Industrial Revolutions of the 18th and 19th centuries brought great changes. New machines were invented and lots of towns, factories, canals, steamships and railways were built

THE ROMANS
43–410 AD

THE ANGLO-SAXONS
About 400–1066

THE VIKINGS
About 800–1042

43 years after the birth of Christ (AD), Britain was invaded by Romans from Italy. They conquered England and Wales, built grand towns and villas, strong forts and long, straight roads.

After the Romans left, England was overrun by Anglo-Saxons from northern Europe and split up into several rival kingdoms. Many Britons fled to Cornwall, Wales, Scotland and Ireland.

Fierce Viking warriors from Scandinavia raided Britain next in dragon-ships, and settled mainly in the east. The Saxon king, Alfred the Great, stopped them from taking over England in 878.

THE TUDORS
1485 – 1603

In 1485, the Lancastrian leader, Henry Tudor, won the Wars of the Roses. These were fought between the Lancastrians (whose badge was a red rose) and the Yorkists (whose badge was a white rose).

Henry Tudor's son, Henry VIII, broke with the Roman Catholic Church in 1534 because the Pope would not let him divorce the first of his six wives. Two less fortunate wives had their heads chopped off.

Elizabeth I was the last Tudor. During her long reign, daring sea captains explored the world and fought off the Spanish navy, the Armada. She was succeeded by Stuart kings and queens.

THE VICTORIAN AGE
1837–1901

THE 20TH CENTURY

Workers, including young children, laboured long hours for very little pay. Some set up trade unions to fight for better living and working conditions. Gradually, new laws were passed to improve these.

Under Queen Victoria, Britain continued to build a huge empire overseas and fought wars to protect its trade and territory. Most countries under British rule won independence this century.

In the last 100 years, women have won the right to vote and social conditions have improved for most people. After fighting in two World Wars, Britain is now forging closer links with Europe.

London

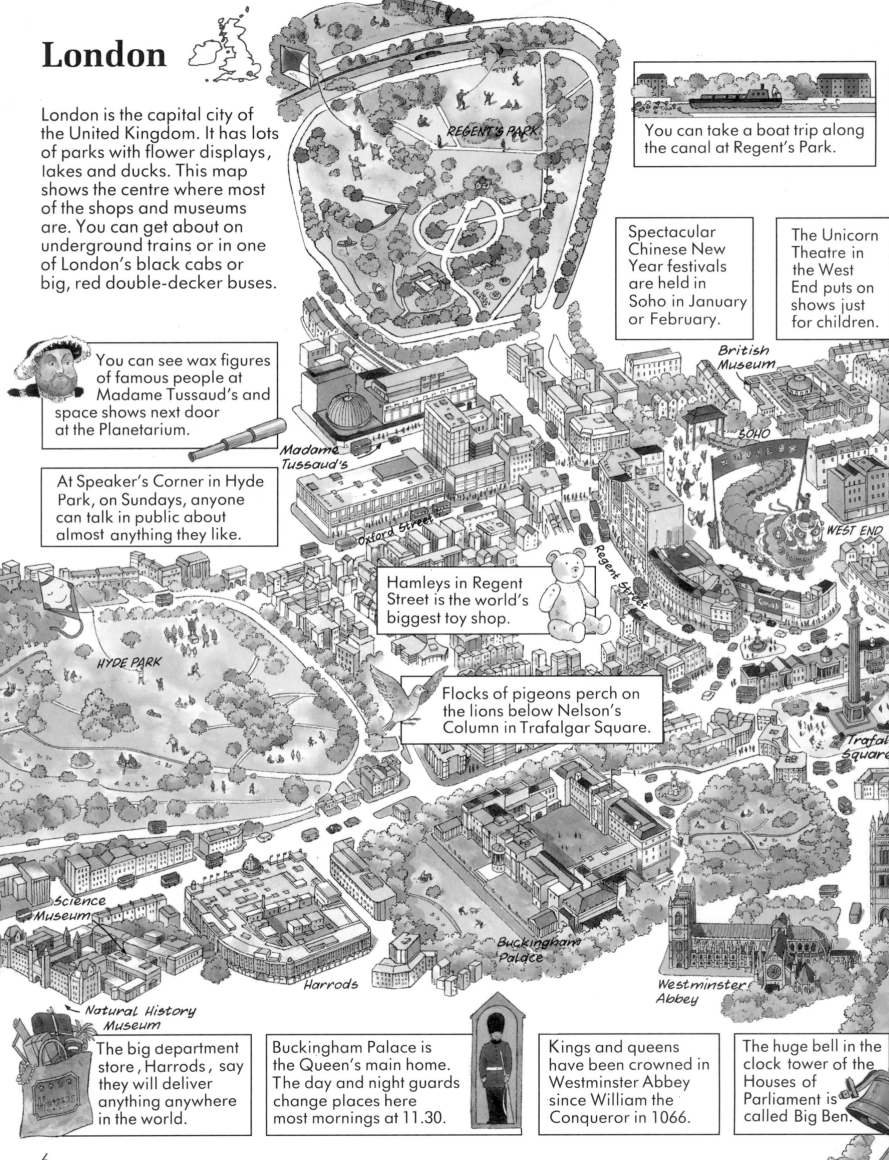

London is the capital city of the United Kingdom. It has lots of parks with flower displays, lakes and ducks. This map shows the centre where most of the shops and museums are. You can get about on underground trains or in one of London's black cabs or big, red double-decker buses.

REGENT'S PARK

You can take a boat trip along the canal at Regent's Park.

Spectacular Chinese New Year festivals are held in Soho in January or February.

The Unicorn Theatre in the West End puts on shows just for children.

British Museum

SOHO

WEST END

You can see wax figures of famous people at Madame Tussaud's and space shows next door at the Planetarium.

At Speaker's Corner in Hyde Park, on Sundays, anyone can talk in public about almost anything they like.

Madame Tussaud's

Oxford Street

Regent Street

Hamleys in Regent Street is the world's biggest toy shop.

HYDE PARK

Flocks of pigeons perch on the lions below Nelson's Column in Trafalgar Square.

Trafalgar Square

Science Museum

Buckingham Palace

Westminster Abbey

Natural History Museum

Harrods

The big department store, Harrods, say they will deliver anything anywhere in the world.

Buckingham Palace is the Queen's main home. The day and night guards change places here most mornings at 11.30.

Kings and queens have been crowned in Westminster Abbey since William the Conqueror in 1066.

The huge bell in the clock tower of the Houses of Parliament is called Big Ben.

London's museums

London has lots of interesting museums to visit. Many are housed in magnificent old buildings.

Some museums can give you activity sheets of things to see and do inside.

The British Museum has ancient statues and objects from around the world.

The Museum of London has the Lord Mayor's coach and displays on London's past.

The Natural History Museum has skeletons and robotic models of dinosaurs.

You can find out how a space rocket works at the Science Museum.

There are exciting things going on to do with film at the Museum of the Moving Image.

Covent Garden has craft stalls and open-air entertainment.

The Whispering Gallery in St Paul's Cathedral echoes back whispers.

Britain's Crown Jewels are kept in the Tower of London.

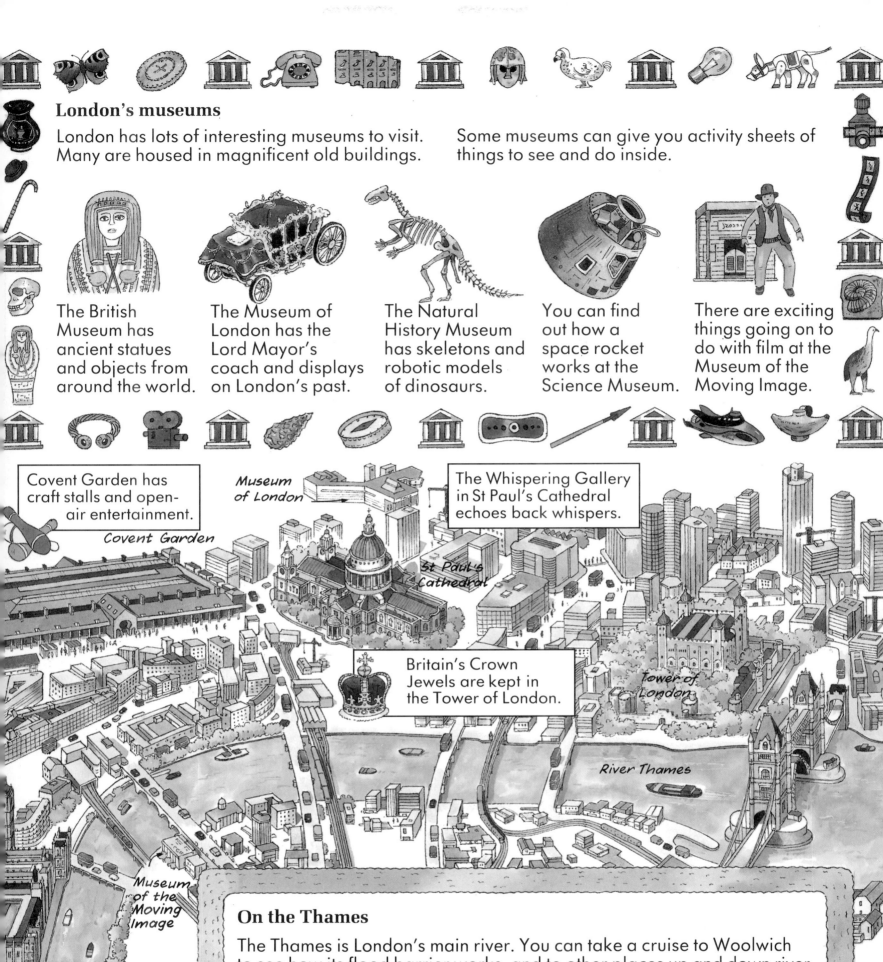

Covent Garden

Museum of London

St Paul's Cathedral

Tower of London

River Thames

Museum of the Moving Image

On the Thames

The Thames is London's main river. You can take a cruise to Woolwich to see how its flood barrier works, and to other places up and down river.

You can try losing yourself in the maze at Hampton Court.

At Greenwich, you can climb aboard the ship, the Cutty Sark.

Kew Gardens has big, steamy greenhouses with tropical plants.

The West Country

The south-west corner of England is known as the West Country. It is lined with sandy beaches and rugged cliffs and the sea is warmed by the Gulf Stream. Inland, narrow lanes wind their way through rolling fields, hills and moors. People come here for the sunny weather and gorgeous scenery.

Clovelly is a pretty fishing village. At the Milky Way farm nearby, you can cuddle the animals and milk a cow.

Cornish festivals

Cornwall celebrates the coming of summer each May with two spring festivals.

Helston is decked with flowers as elegant people dance the "Furry Dance" in and out of shops and houses.

A man dressed as a horse called the "Obby Oss" leads the dancing and singing through Padstow.

ATLANTIC OCEAN

The north coast is more rugged than the south. Surfers ride the breakers which roll in from the Atlantic Ocean.

It is said that people called wreckers once guided storm-tossed ships onto rocks with lights, to rob them as they sank.

A Cornish giant called Bedruthan is said to have used the massive rocks, Bedruthan Steps, as stepping stones.

Clovelly

Tintagel

Padstow

Bedruthan Steps

The rocky cliffs at Land's End mark the most westerly tip of mainland Britain.

CORNWALL

ISLES OF SCILLY

Helston

Goonhilly Downs

Land's End

St Michael's Mount

Tresco

Smugglers used to sneak in tobacco, lace and brandy from France to secret coves along the coast.

Tresco is one of the Isles of Scilly off Land's End. It has long, silver beaches and a tropical garden.

You can go down Poldark Tin Mine near Helston and post a card from Britain's deepest underground letter box.

The dish aerials at Goonhilly Satellite Earth Station send telephone calls and television pictures around the world.

8

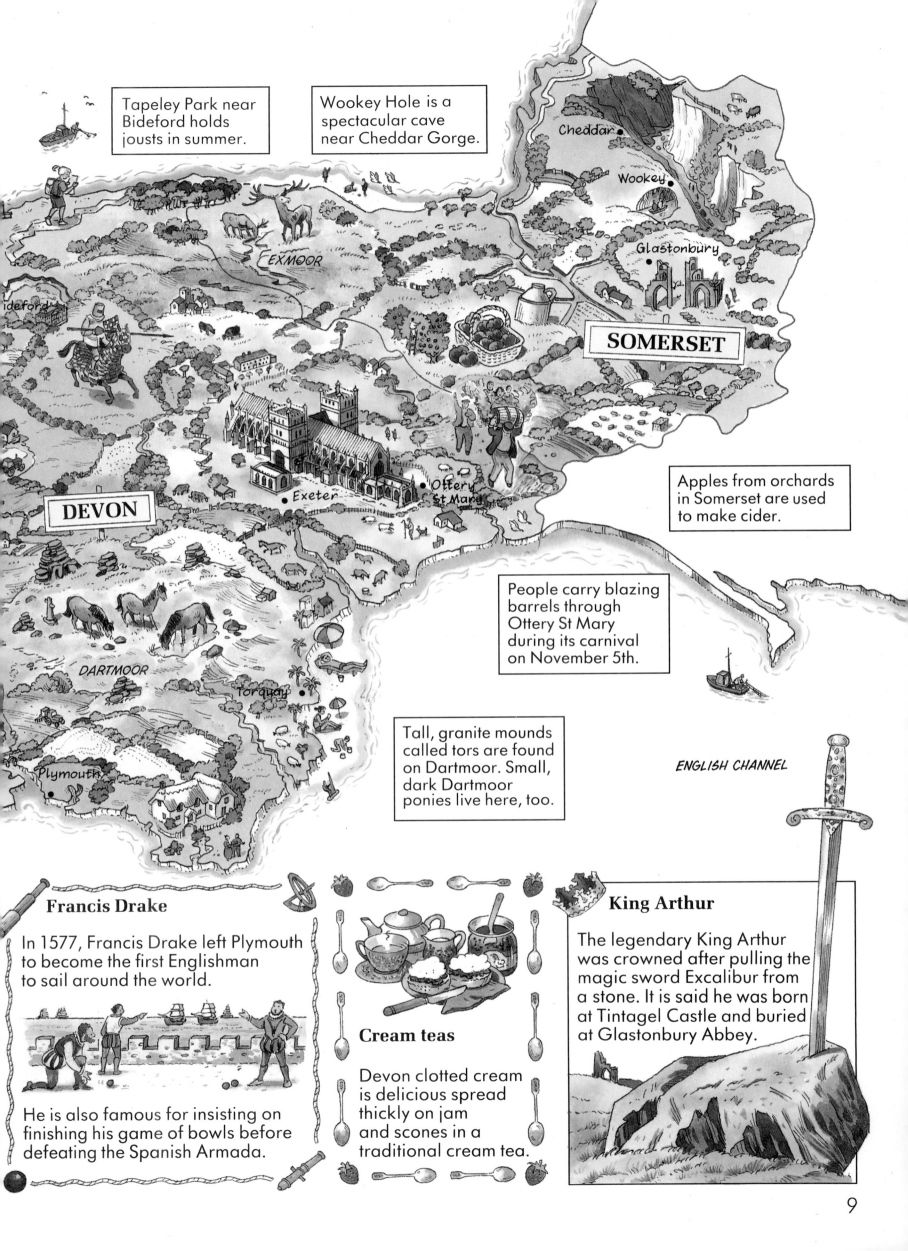

Tapeley Park near Bideford holds jousts in summer.

Wookey Hole is a spectacular cave near Cheddar Gorge.

Cheddar

Wookey

Glastonbury

EXMOOR

SOMERSET

DEVON

Exeter

Ottery St Mary

Bideford

Apples from orchards in Somerset are used to make cider.

People carry blazing barrels through Ottery St Mary during its carnival on November 5th.

DARTMOOR

Torquay

ENGLISH CHANNEL

Plymouth

Tall, granite mounds called tors are found on Dartmoor. Small, dark Dartmoor ponies live here, too.

Francis Drake

In 1577, Francis Drake left Plymouth to become the first Englishman to sail around the world.

He is also famous for insisting on finishing his game of bowls before defeating the Spanish Armada.

Cream teas

Devon clotted cream is delicious spread thickly on jam and scones in a traditional cream tea.

King Arthur

The legendary King Arthur was crowned after pulling the magic sword Excalibur from a stone. It is said he was born at Tintagel Castle and buried at Glastonbury Abbey.

The South Coast

The south of England is lined with dramatic white cliffs, wide beaches and popular seaside resorts. Early invaders landed along the coast nearest Europe. This is still the first part of Britain most people see as they land at one of its busy air or sea ports.

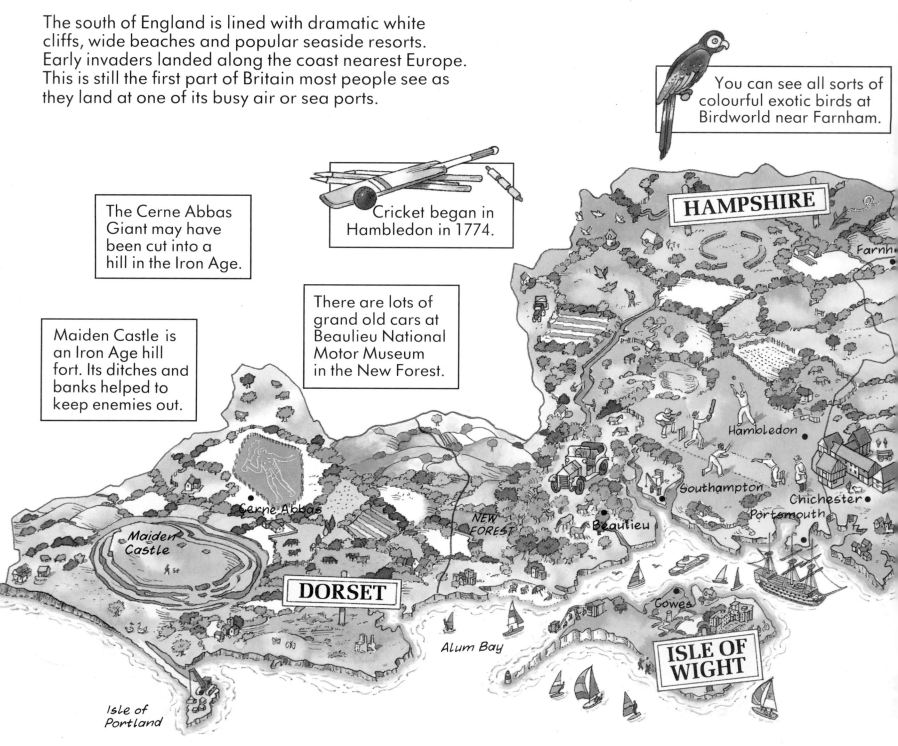

You can see all sorts of colourful exotic birds at Birdworld near Farnham.

Cricket began in Hambledon in 1774.

The Cerne Abbas Giant may have been cut into a hill in the Iron Age.

There are lots of grand old cars at Beaulieu National Motor Museum in the New Forest.

Maiden Castle is an Iron Age hill fort. Its ditches and banks helped to keep enemies out.

HAMPSHIRE

DORSET

ISLE OF WIGHT

Maiden Castle

Cerne Abbas

NEW FOREST

Beaulieu

Southampton

Hambledon

Chichester

Portsmouth

Farnh

Cowes

Alum Bay

Isle of Portland

The Channel Islands

The Channel Islands lie near France. They became part of Britain at the time of the Norman conquest. During Jersey's "Battle of Flowers" festival in August, people decorate floats with tons of flowers.

GUERNSEY

JERSEY

In August, hundreds of yachts take part in international races at Cowes on the Isle of Wight.

Historic buildings have been rebuilt at the Weald and Downland Museum near Chichester.

A chairlift goes down to Alum Bay on the Isle of Wight, where the sands are all different colours.

At Portsmouth, you can find out how the ship, the Mary Rose, was raised after 437 years under the sea.

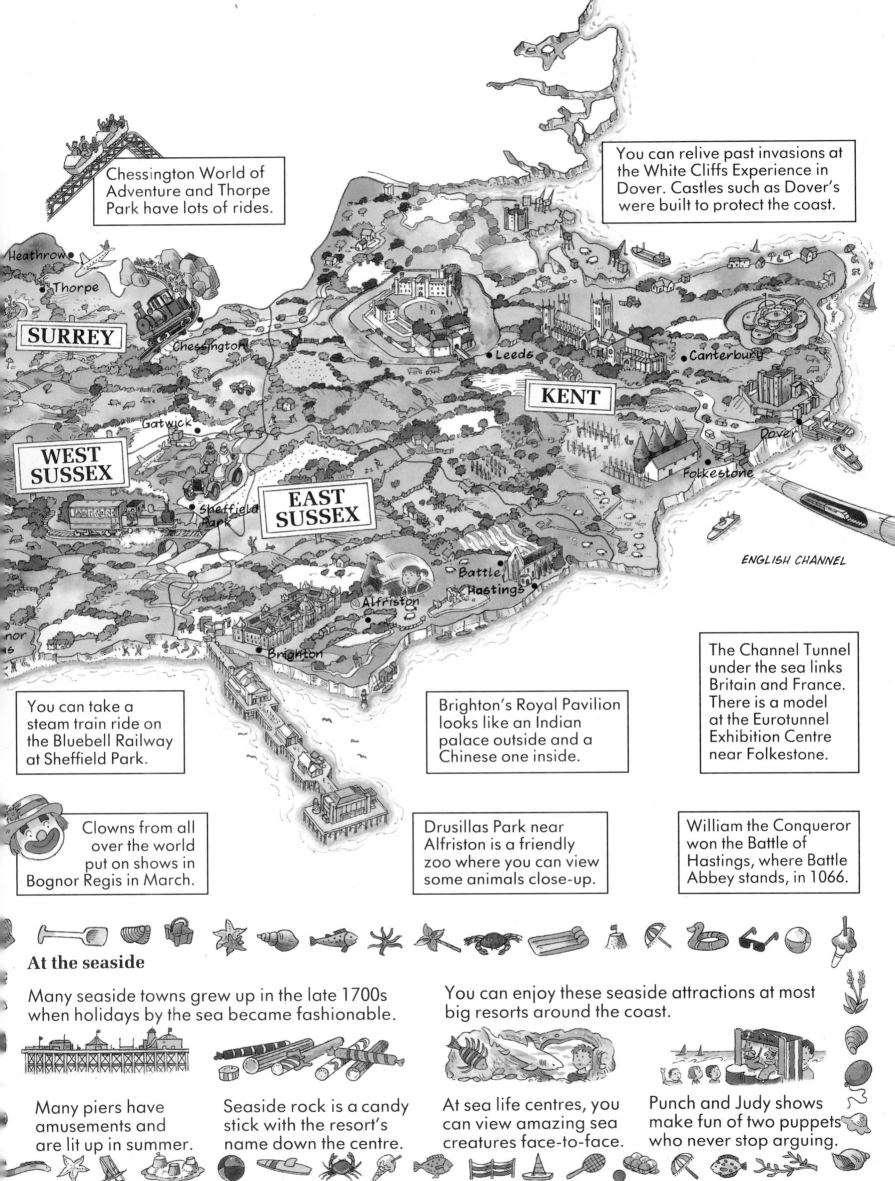

Chessington World of Adventure and Thorpe Park have lots of rides.

You can relive past invasions at the White Cliffs Experience in Dover. Castles such as Dover's were built to protect the coast.

Heathrow

Thorpe

SURREY

Chessington

Gatwick

WEST SUSSEX

Sheffield Park

EAST SUSSEX

Leeds

Canterbury

KENT

Dover

Folkestone

Battle
Hastings

Alfriston

Brighton

ENGLISH CHANNEL

You can take a steam train ride on the Bluebell Railway at Sheffield Park.

Brighton's Royal Pavilion looks like an Indian palace outside and a Chinese one inside.

The Channel Tunnel under the sea links Britain and France. There is a model at the Eurotunnel Exhibition Centre near Folkestone.

Clowns from all over the world put on shows in Bognor Regis in March.

Drusillas Park near Alfriston is a friendly zoo where you can view some animals close-up.

William the Conqueror won the Battle of Hastings, where Battle Abbey stands, in 1066.

At the seaside

Many seaside towns grew up in the late 1700s when holidays by the sea became fashionable.

You can enjoy these seaside attractions at most big resorts around the coast.

Many piers have amusements and are lit up in summer.

Seaside rock is a candy stick with the resort's name down the centre.

At sea life centres, you can view amazing sea creatures face-to-face.

Punch and Judy shows make fun of two puppets who never stop arguing.

11

The heart of England

There are many ancient sites and historic houses in this part of England. People enjoy boating on the River Thames which flows through the area, and walking and riding over the Cotswold and Chiltern hills.

There is a wildlife park at Burford, and others at Longleat, Whipsnade Windsor and Woburn.

An Iron Age tribe may have cut the Uffington White Horse to show they ruled the area.

On the Forest of Dean Sculpture Trail, you will see sculptures of animals and things to do with the forest.

At the Wildfowl and Wetland Centre in Slimbridge, you can spy all kinds of wild birds from hidden look-outs.

Clifton Suspension Bridge in Bristol was designed by the engineer, Isambard Kingdom Brunel.

In 1840, the first stamped letter was posted from what is now the Bath Postal Museum. A Penny Black stamp was used.

POSTAGE
ONE PENNY

The stone rings at Stonehenge and Avebury are over 3500 years old. Stonehenge may have been used to worship the sun and mark the seasons.

GLOUCESTERSHIRE

COTSWOLD HILLS

Burford

FOREST OF DEAN

Slimbridge

WILTSHIRE

Uffington

Avebury

West Kennet

Bristol

AVON

Bath

Longleat House

Stonehenge

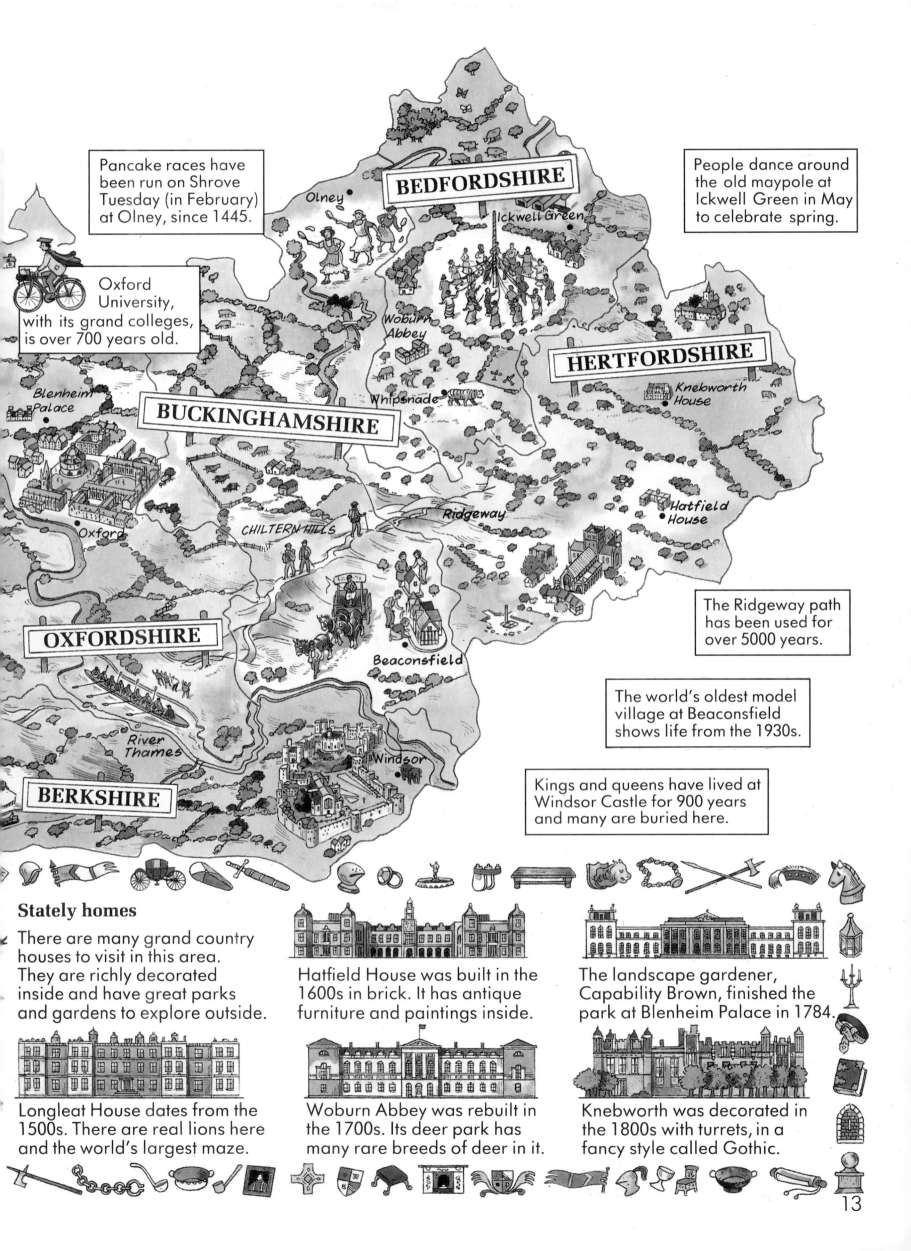

BEDFORDSHIRE

Olney

Ickwell Green

Pancake races have been run on Shrove Tuesday (in February) at Olney, since 1445.

People dance around the old maypole at Ickwell Green in May to celebrate spring.

Oxford University, with its grand colleges, is over 700 years old.

Woburn Abbey

HERTFORDSHIRE

Knebworth House

Blenheim Palace

BUCKINGHAMSHIRE

Whipsnade

Oxford

CHILTERN HILLS

Ridgeway

Hatfield House

OXFORDSHIRE

Beaconsfield

The Ridgeway path has been used for over 5000 years.

River Thames

The world's oldest model village at Beaconsfield shows life from the 1930s.

Windsor

BERKSHIRE

Kings and queens have lived at Windsor Castle for 900 years and many are buried here.

Stately homes

There are many grand country houses to visit in this area. They are richly decorated inside and have great parks and gardens to explore outside.

Hatfield House was built in the 1600s in brick. It has antique furniture and paintings inside.

The landscape gardener, Capability Brown, finished the park at Blenheim Palace in 1784.

Longleat House dates from the 1500s. There are real lions here and the world's largest maze.

Woburn Abbey was rebuilt in the 1700s. Its deer park has many rare breeds of deer in it.

Knebworth was decorated in the 1800s with turrets, in a fancy style called Gothic.

East Anglia

East Anglia is the round part of eastern England which juts out into the North Sea. It is separated from Lincolnshire by a wide inlet called the Wash. The rich farmland around the Wash is called the Fens. All sorts of grain, vegetables, fruit and flowers grow here. The Fens are very flat and on clear evenings you can see brilliant sunsets spread far across the open skies.

Draining the Fens

The Fens were once marshes. In the 1600s, Dutch engineers dug channels through them to let water drain into the sea. Windmills, steam engines and electric pumps were later used to pump out more water. You can see what the Fens used to look like at Wicken Fen, which has never been drained.

Buried treasure

Two treasure hoards have been found in Suffolk. They are now in the British Museum in London.

Lots of Roman silverware was ploughed up near Mildenhall in 1946. It had been buried 1600 years ago in times of danger.

The Sutton Hoo treasure, buried in a Saxon ship in the 600s, was found near Woodbridge in 1939.

King John's treasure, loaded in wagons, sank in quicksands in the Wash in 1216. Treasure hunters are still trying to find it.

Reeds from the Broads are used to thatch roofs with wavy patterns.

Peat was once dug from marshes in Norfolk. The flooded pits form the lakes of the Norfolk Broads.

The magnificent cathedral at Lincoln has three towers.

LINCOLNSHIRE

The scientist, Isaac Newton, was born at Woolsthorpe Manor near Grantham in 1642.

Lincoln

Boston

Grantham

NORFOLK BROADS

THE WASH

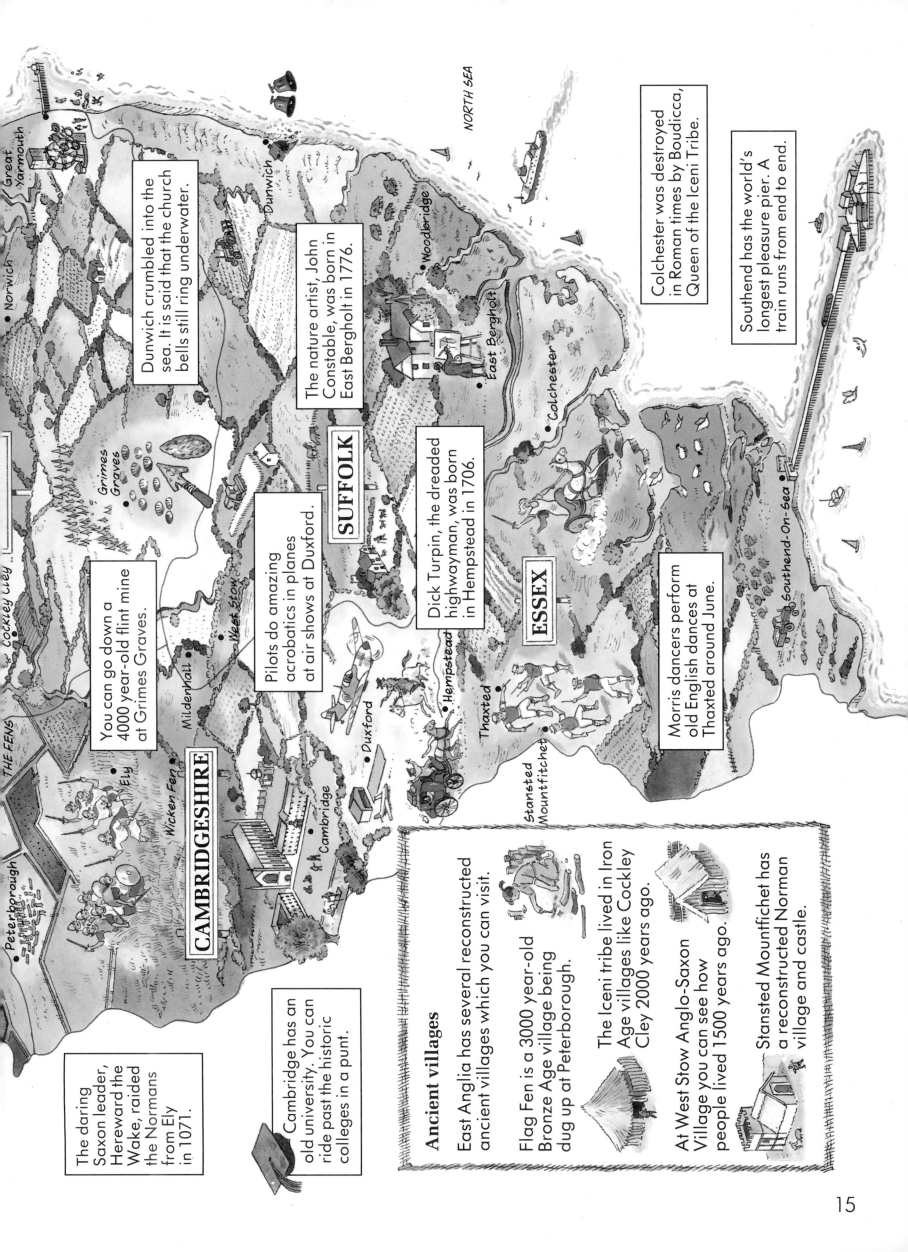

NORTH SEA

Dunwich crumbled into the sea. It is said that the church bells still ring underwater.

The nature artist, John Constable, was born in East Bergholt in 1776.

Colchester was destroyed in Roman times by Boudicca, Queen of the Iceni Tribe.

Southend has the world's longest pleasure pier. A train runs from end to end.

SUFFOLK

You can go down a 4000 year-old flint mine at Grimes Graves.

Pilots do amazing acrobatics in planes at air shows at Duxford.

Dick Turpin, the dreaded highwayman, was born in Hempstead in 1706.

ESSEX

Morris dancers perform old English dances at Thaxted around June.

CAMBRIDGESHIRE

The daring Saxon leader, Hereward the Wake, raided the Normans from Ely in 1071.

Cambridge has an old university. You can ride past the historic colleges in a punt.

Ancient villages

East Anglia has several reconstructed ancient villages which you can visit.

Flag Fen is a 3000 year-old Bronze Age village being dug up at Peterborough.

The Iceni tribe lived in Iron Age villages like Cockley Cley 2000 years ago.

At West Stow Anglo-Saxon Village you can see how people lived 1500 years ago.

Stansted Mountfichet has a reconstructed Norman village and castle.

Great Yarmouth

Norwich

Dunwich

Woodbridge

East Bergholt

Colchester

Southend-On-Sea

Grimes Graves

Cockley Cley

West Stow

Mildenhall

Ely

Wicken Fen

THE FENS

Cambridge

Duxford

Hempstead

Thaxted

Stansted Mountfichet

Peterborough

The Midlands

The Midlands lie between the north and south of England and many battles have been fought on their hills and plains. The Industrial Revolution began here in Coalbrookdale in 1709, when Abraham Darby invented a better way to make iron. For hundreds of years, coal, iron, lead and clay have been dug out of the ground and used in local industry.

Made in the Midlands

Many places in the Midlands are known for the things that are made there. You can visit museums and factories in these areas to see how things used to be made and how they are made now.

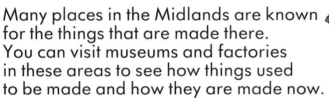 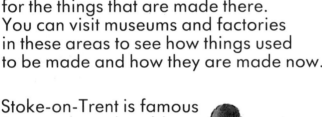

Stoke-on-Trent is famous for pottery such as blue and white Wedgwood china. You can see potters at work at the Gladstone Pottery Museum here.

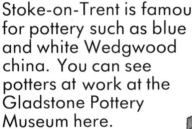

 Glass has been made around Stourbridge for 400 years. You can visit glassworks in the area to watch crystal being blown and cut by hand.

Leicester, Nottingham, Loughborough and Northampton are known in turn for stockings, lace, bells and shoes. Nottingham's Lace Hall has fine pieces of lace.

  Cars, tyres, chocolate and other things are made in Birmingham and the West Midlands. The story of chocolate is told at Cadbury World in Birmingham.

16

At Ironbridge Gorge, you can visit old factories, a Victorian town and the world's first iron bridge.

King Offa marked the edge of his Saxon kingdom with a long ditch called Offa's Dyke.

Offa's Dyke

Sto -on- Tren

Shrewsbury

Coalbrookdale
Ironbridge

SHROPSHIRE

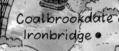

Stourbridge

Ludlow

Acton Scott Historic Working Farm near Ludlow shows farm life from 100 years ago.

HEREFORD AND WORCESTERSHIRE

In the Peak District, you can ride a cable car down the Heights of Abraham and explore caves at Castleton.

DERBYSHIRE

Britain's largest theme park, Alton Towers, has over 125 thrilling rides.

STAFFORDSHIRE

Abbots Bromley holds an ancient Horn Dance in September.

NOTTINGHAMSHIRE

· Nottingham

LEICESTERSHIRE

· Leicester

Henry Tudor won the final battle of the Wars of the Roses at Bosworth in 1495.

Market Bosworth

Loughborough

WEST MIDLANDS

Birmingham

NORTHAMPTONSHIRE

· Naseby

· Northampton

WARWICKSHIRE

Warwick

Stratford-upon-Avon

You can walk among tropical butterflies at Stratford's Butterfly Jungle and Safari.

You can climb up Warwick Castle's towers and deep down into its gruesome dungeons.

Robin Hood

The legendary outlaw, Robin Hood, lived in Sherwood forest 750 years ago. He and his men are said to have hidden in a tree here called the Major Oak.

Nottingham's Tales of Robin Hood exhibition tells how he wooed Maid Marian and waged war on his arch-enemy, the wicked Sheriff of Nottingham.

Oliver Cromwell won the decisive battle of the Civil War when he defeated King Charles I at Naseby in 1645.

Shakespeare

The great playwright, William Shakespeare, was born in Stratford in 1564. His plays are acted here and in theatres all over the world.

You can see the childhood home of his wife, Anne Hathaway, and the World of Shakespeare exhibition. People celebrate his birthday here in April.

17

The North West

The main cities in the North West are Manchester and Liverpool. They grew into busy ports 200 years ago when the cotton industry was based here. Above this manufacturing area lie the lakes and mountains of the Lake District, where people come to relax.

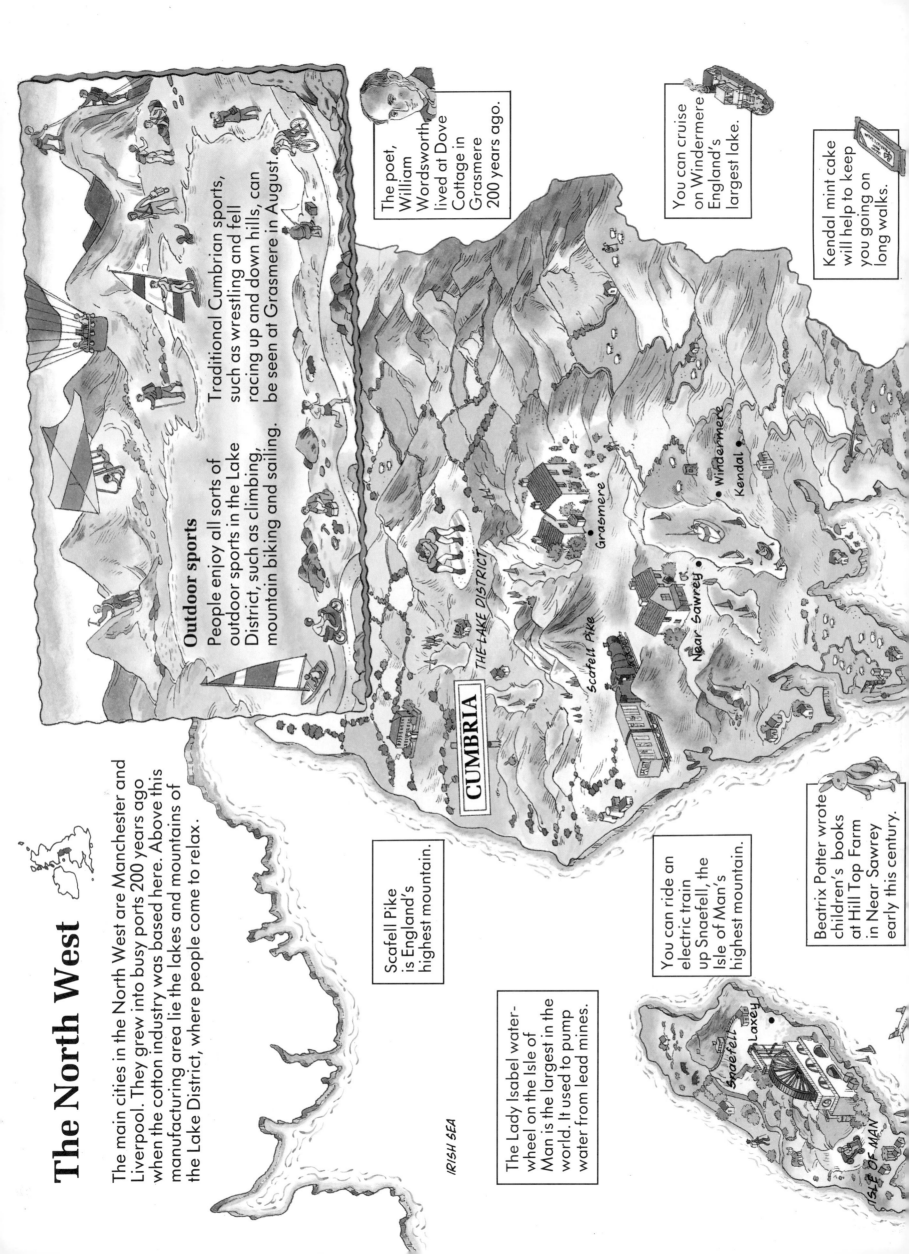

Outdoor sports

People enjoy all sorts of outdoor sports in the Lake District, such as climbing, mountain biking and sailing.

Traditional Cumbrian sports, such as wrestling and fell racing up and down hills, can be seen at Grasmere in August.

The poet, William Wordsworth lived at Dove Cottage in Grasmere 200 years ago.

You can cruise on Windermere England's largest lake.

Kendal mint cake will help to keep you going on long walks.

Scafell Pike is England's highest mountain.

You can ride an electric train up Snaefell, the Isle of Man's highest mountain.

Beatrix Potter wrote children's books at Hill Top Farm in Near Sawrey early this century.

The Lady Isabel waterwheel on the Isle of Man is the largest in the world. It used to pump water from lead mines.

CUMBRIA

THE LAKE DISTRICT

Scafell Pike

Grasmere

Windermere

Kendal

Near Sawrey

IRISH SEA

Snaefell

Laxey

ISLE OF MAN

LANCASHIRE

GREATER MANCHESTER

• Manchester

MERSEYSIDE

Liverpool

CHESHIRE

Chorley •

Blackpool

Little Moreton Hall

Wilmslow

Knutsford •
Tatton Park

Jodrell Bank

Congleton

Mow Cop

Ellesmere Port

Mow Cop is a mock ruin with wide views and a path to Little Moreton Hall.

Blackpool has its own tower and pleasure beach. It is lit up in autumn with bright illuminations.

Camelot Theme Park near Chorley has scary rides and medieval entertainment.

Liverpool has an exhibition on the Beatles pop group, who came from here.

At Tatton Park, you can see how people have lived and worked here through the ages.

At Jodrell Bank, you can find out how a giant radio telescope receives radio waves from space.

Cotton mills

Lancashire was the centre of Britain's cotton industry from the 1700s and many giant machines were invented here to spin and weave cotton.

You can see how they worked at the Quarry Bank Mill in Wilmslow. Young children were once made to work here six days a week by harsh mill owners.

Canals and boats

Britain's first canals were also built in this area over 200 years ago. They were used to carry coal, cotton and other things around the country.

You can climb aboard some of the old horse-drawn boats at the Boat Museum at Ellesmere Port, and sail on others on canals around Britain.

The North East

The North East has many big ports and cities. These grew up around important fishing, wool, coal-mining, iron and steel industries in the area. There are also rolling hills, windswept moors, forests, lakes and long, sandy beaches.

Cathedrals and abbeys

This area has many ruined abbeys where nuns and monks once lived, and several cathedrals.

You can climb up Durham Cathedral for great views of the city and castle.

Celtic monks built a priory on Lindisfarne (or Holy Island) 1300 years ago.

Fountains Abbey is a fantastic ruin to explore with a lovely water garden nearby.

York Minster has 128 stained glass windows. It took over 250 years to build.

Railways

Many early railways were built in this area. The first steam-powered public railway ran from Stockton to Darlington in 1825.

It opened with George Stephenson's steam engine, the Locomotion, which is now at Darlington. York also has a Railway Museum.

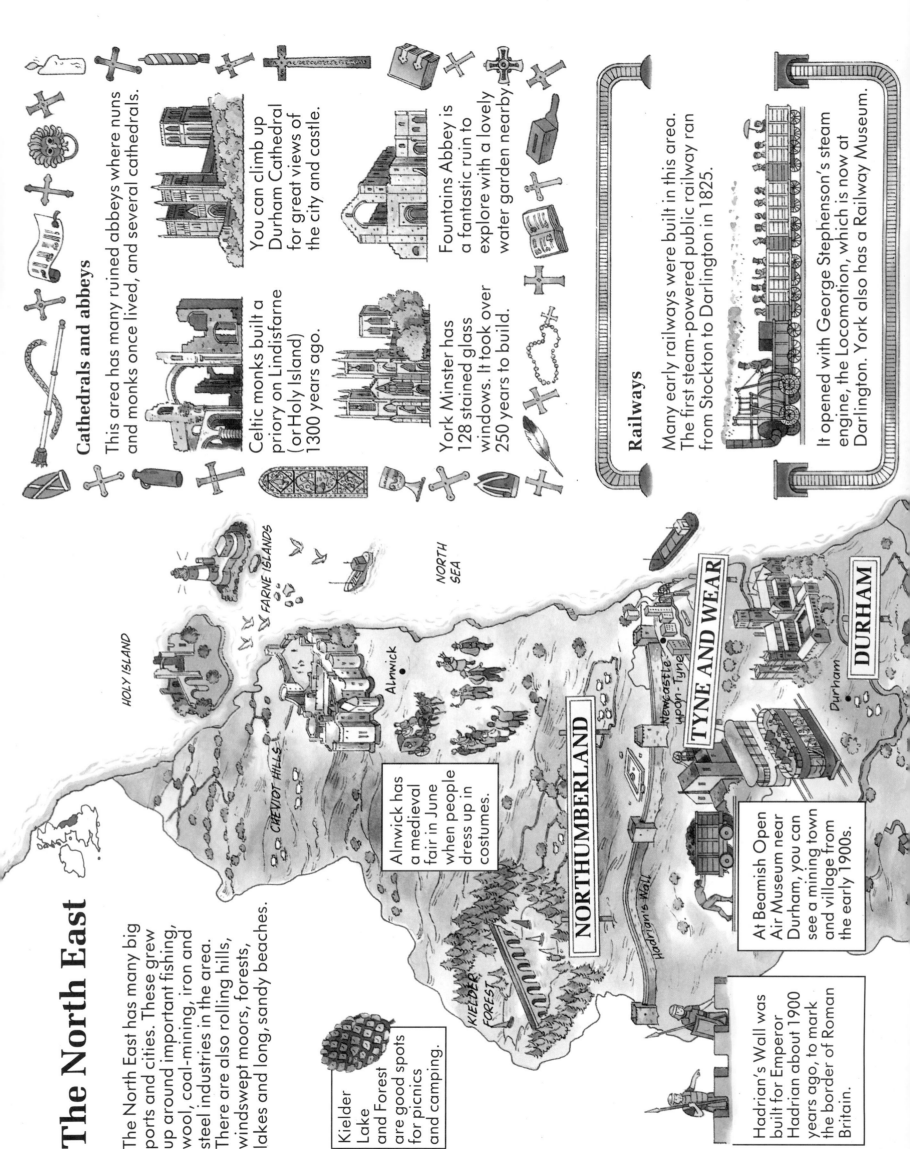

HOLY ISLAND

FARNE ISLANDS

NORTH SEA

CHEVIOT HILLS

Alnwick

Alnwick has a medieval fair in June when people dress up in costumes.

Kielder Lake and Forest are good spots for picnics and camping.

KIELDER FOREST

NORTHUMBERLAND

Hadrian's Wall

Newcastle-upon-Tyne

TYNE AND WEAR

Durham

DURHAM

At Beamish Open Air Museum near Durham, you can see a mining town and village from the early 1900s.

Hadrian's Wall was built for Emperor Hadrian about 1900 years ago, to mark the border of Roman Britain.

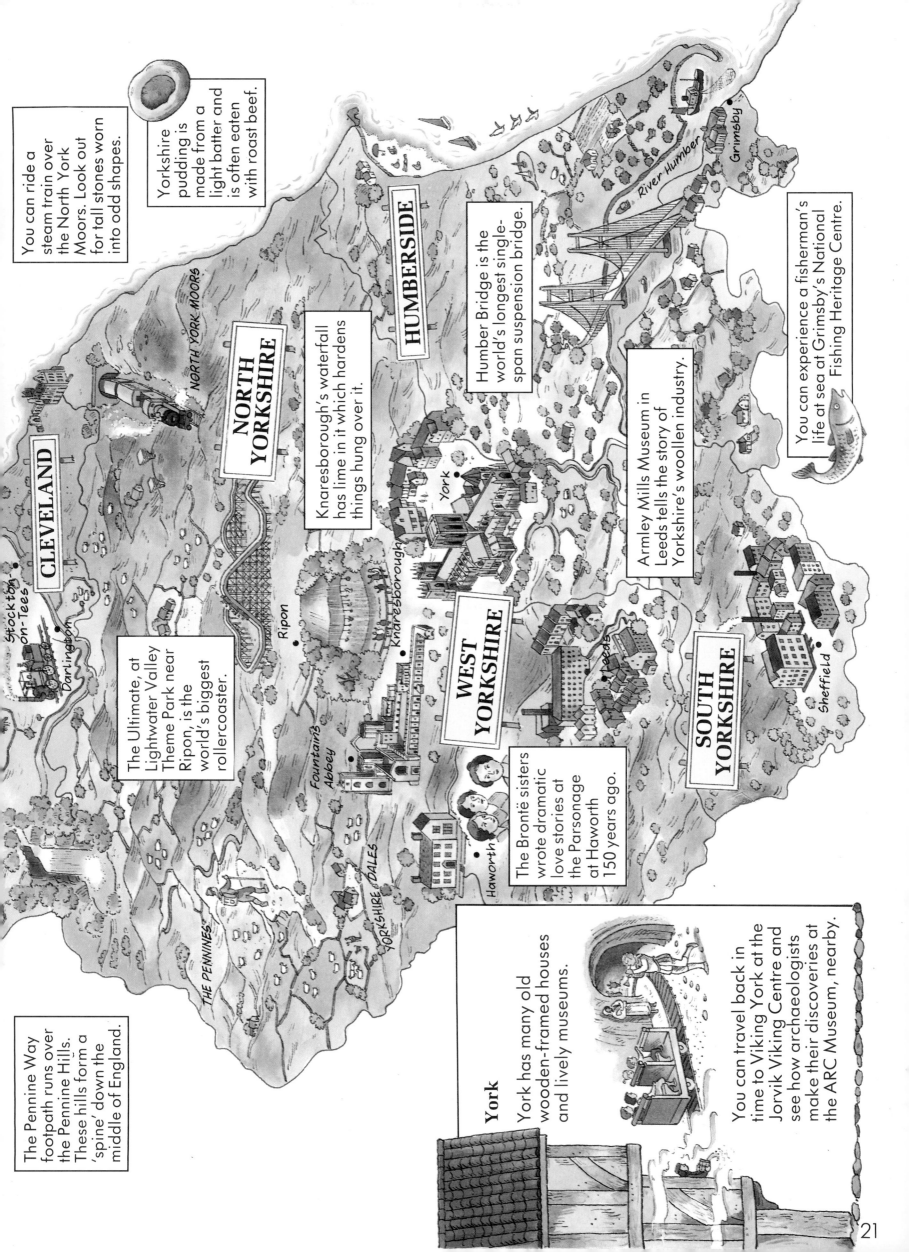

You can ride a steam train over the North York Moors. Look out for tall stones worn into odd shapes.

Yorkshire pudding is made from a light batter and is often eaten with roast beef.

HUMBERSIDE

NORTH YORKSHIRE

Knaresborough's waterfall has lime in it which hardens things hung over it.

Humber Bridge is the world's longest single-span suspension bridge.

CLEVELAND

You can experience a fisherman's life at sea at Grimsby's National Fishing Heritage Centre.

Armley Mills Museum in Leeds tells the story of Yorkshire's woollen industry.

The Ultimate, at Lightwater Valley Theme Park near Ripon, is the world's biggest rollercoaster.

WEST YORKSHIRE

SOUTH YORKSHIRE

The Brontë sisters wrote dramatic love stories at the Parsonage at Haworth 150 years ago.

The Pennine Way footpath runs over the Pennine Hills. These hills form a 'spine' down the middle of England.

York

York has many old wooden-framed houses and lively museums.

You can travel back in time to Viking York at the Jorvik Viking Centre and see how archaeologists make their discoveries at the ARC Museum, nearby.

NORTH YORK MOORS

Stockton-on-Tees

Darlington

Ripon

Fountains Abbey

Knaresborough

York

Leeds

Sheffield

Grimsby

River Humber

YORKSHIRE DALES

THE PENNINES

Haworth

Wales

Wales is a hilly country with high mountains and deep valleys. For hundreds of years it was made up of separate Celtic kingdoms which were invaded in turn by the Romans, Normans and English. It was joined to England by 1543. Welsh culture is celebrated at the Royal National Eisteddfod of Wales, a contest in music and dance which is held at a different place each year.

The town of Llanfair PG has the longest name in Britain. Its full name is: Llanfairpwllgwyngyllgogerychwyrndrobwllllantysiliogogogoch.

At the Museum of the North in Llanberis, you can find out all about people, events and industries in Welsh history.

You can see terrible dragons, knights, giants, goblins and witches from Welsh folklore at the Knights Cavern in Rhyl.

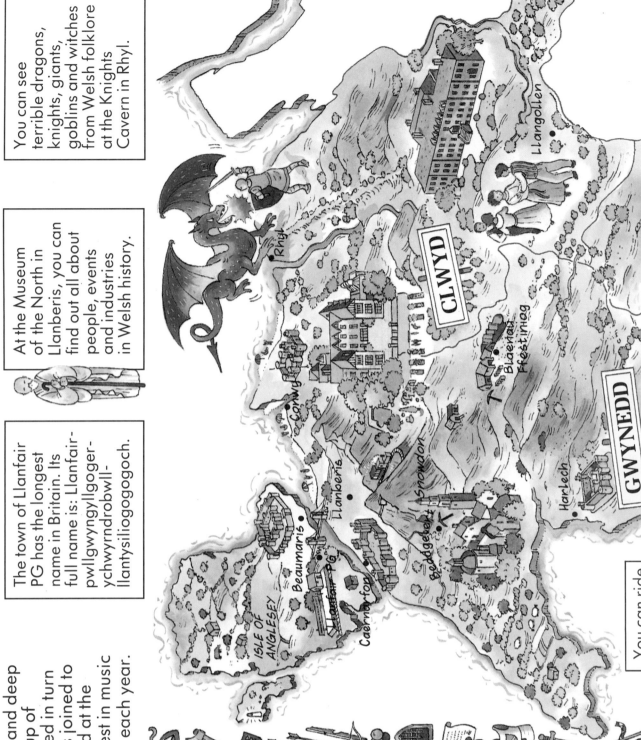

CLWYD

GWYNEDD

Llangollen holds an International Musical Eisteddfod in July.

You can ride a train up Snowdon, the highest mountain in Wales.

Castles

Many castles were built in Wales during clashes between the Welsh and English in the Middle Ages. King Edward I built these four in the late 1200s after defeating the Welsh leader, Llywelyn the Great.

Beaumaris' moat and battlements helped to keep enemies out.

You can walk along the high walls of Conwy town and castle.

There are great views from Caernarfon's lofty towers.

Harlech rises up from a rocky crag with steps plunging down.

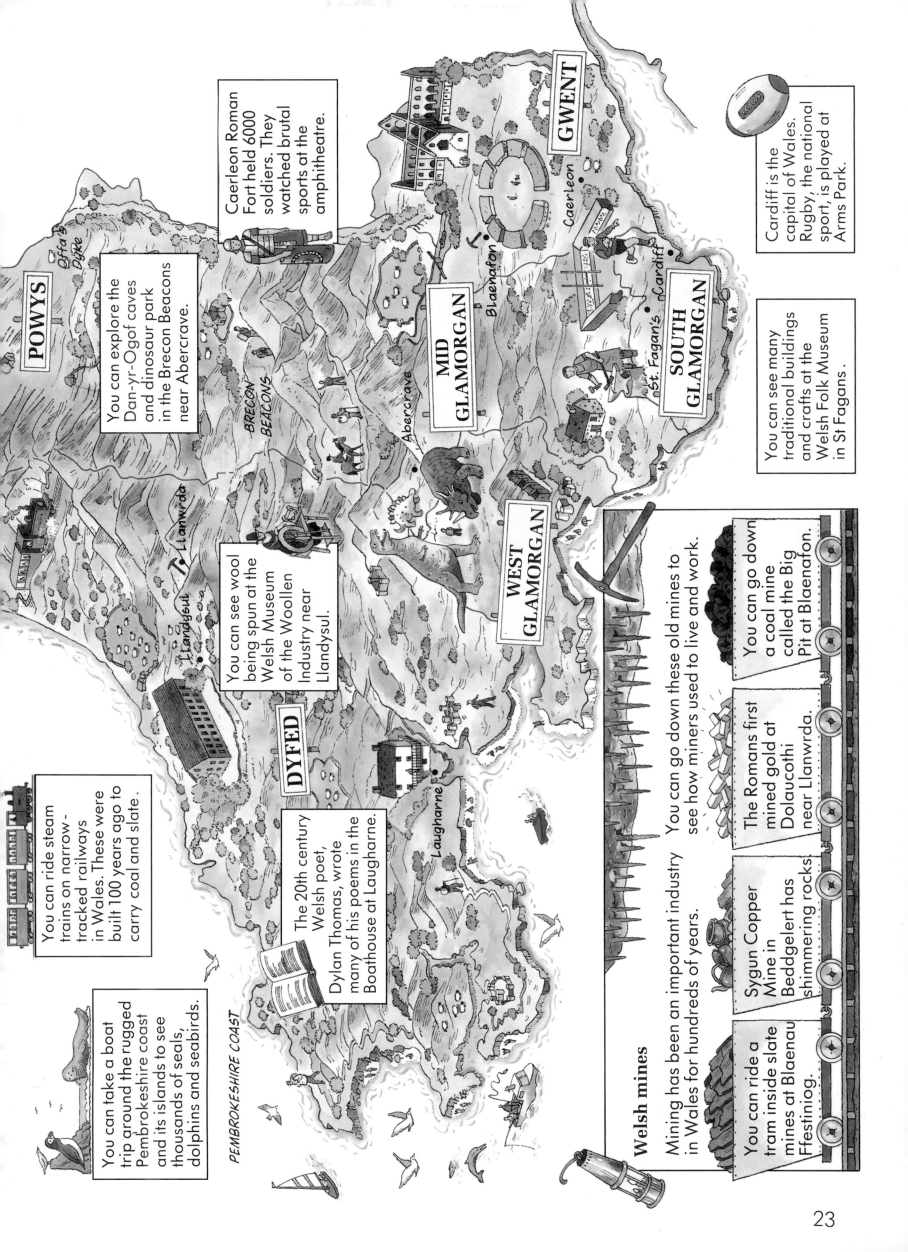

POWYS

GWENT

Caerleon Roman Fort held 6000 soldiers. They watched brutal sports at the amphitheatre.

You can explore the Dan-yr-Ogof caves and dinosaur park in the Brecon Beacons near Abercrave.

Cardiff is the capital of Wales. Rugby, the national sport, is played at Arms Park.

Offa's Dyke

MID GLAMORGAN

Caerleon

Blaenafon

BRECON BEACONS

St. Fagan's Cardiff

SOUTH GLAMORGAN

Abercrave

You can see many traditional buildings and crafts at the Welsh Folk Museum in St Fagans.

You can see wool being spun at the Welsh Museum of the Woollen Industry near Llandysul.

Llanwrda

Llandysul

WEST GLAMORGAN

DYFED

You can ride steam trains on narrow-tracked railways in Wales. These were built 100 years ago to carry coal and slate.

The 20th century Welsh poet, Dylan Thomas, wrote many of his poems in the Boathouse at Laugharne.

Laugharne

You take a boat trip around the rugged Pembrokeshire coast and its islands to see thousands of seals, dolphins and seabirds.

PEMBROKESHIRE COAST

Welsh mines

Mining has been an important industry in Wales for hundreds of years.

You can go down these old mines to see how miners used to live and work.

You can go down a coal mine called the Big Pit at Blaenafon.

The Romans first mined gold at Dolaucothi near Llanwrda.

Sygun Copper Mine in Beddgelert has shimmering rocks.

You can ride a tram inside slate mines at Blaenau Ffestiniog.

23

Southern Scotland

Scotland makes up a large part of Britain. The capital city, Edinburgh, is in the south. This area is known as the Lowlands because it has fewer mountains than the north, although it is still very hilly. There are many ruined abbeys and castles along the Border where Scotland and England once fought bitter wars, before they were united under Stuart kings and queens in 1603.

Robert Burns

Robert Burns is Scotland's best-loved poet. He was born in Alloway on January 25th, 1759, and later lived in Dumfries. Both places have Robert Burns Centres.

His birthday is celebrated on Burns Night by Scots all over the world. During the evening, haggis is carried in to the sound of bagpipes and his poems are read out aloud.

Haggis

Scotland's best-known food is haggis, a sheep's stomach stuffed with meat and oats. It is served with mashed potatoes and turnips on special occasions.

Glasgow

STRATHCLYDE

Wanlock

Alloway

You can walk through an old lead mine at Wanlockhead, Scotland's highest village.

You can see shaggy highland cattle and other Scottish farm animals at Blowplain Farm near Dumfries.

DUMFRIES
AND
GALLOWAY

Fishing ports and villages line the coast of Scotland and seals breed offshore.

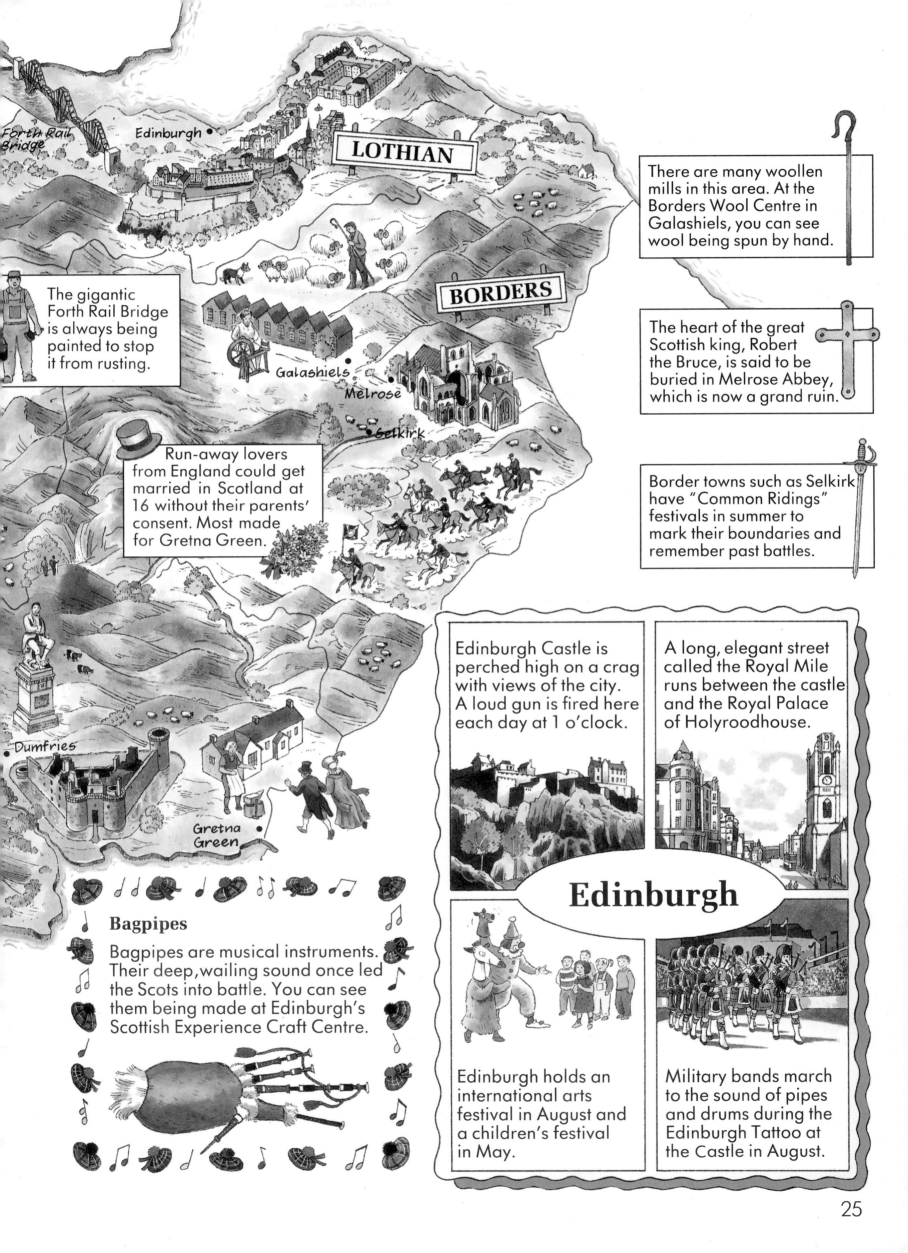

LOTHIAN

BORDERS

Forth Rail Bridge

Edinburgh •

Galashiels

Melrose

Selkirk

Dumfries

Gretna Green

There are many woollen mills in this area. At the Borders Wool Centre in Galashiels, you can see wool being spun by hand.

The gigantic Forth Rail Bridge is always being painted to stop it from rusting.

The heart of the great Scottish king, Robert the Bruce, is said to be buried in Melrose Abbey, which is now a grand ruin.

Run-away lovers from England could get married in Scotland at 16 without their parents' consent. Most made for Gretna Green.

Border towns such as Selkirk have "Common Ridings" festivals in summer to mark their boundaries and remember past battles.

Edinburgh Castle is perched high on a crag with views of the city. A loud gun is fired here each day at 1 o'clock.

A long, elegant street called the Royal Mile runs between the castle and the Royal Palace of Holyroodhouse.

Edinburgh

Edinburgh holds an international arts festival in August and a children's festival in May.

Military bands march to the sound of pipes and drums during the Edinburgh Tattoo at the Castle in August.

Bagpipes

Bagpipes are musical instruments. Their deep, wailing sound once led the Scots into battle. You can see them being made at Edinburgh's Scottish Experience Craft Centre.

Central Scotland

Central Scotland is split into Highlands and Lowlands. The west coast is cut up into islands and long sea inlets and lakes called lochs. Inland, misty mountains sweep down into deep valleys called glens and heather moors. Many of Scotland's industries are based around the east coast which is much flatter. This area also has lots of castles which once belonged to large family groups called clans, who used to feud with each other.

Tartan is a checked cloth traditionally worn by Scots. There are hundreds of patterns from different clans at the Tartans Museum in Comrie.

Highland Games

Highland Games are held throughout Scotland in summer, with bagpipe playing, pipe bands and highland dancing.

You can also watch unusual contests such as "tossing the caber". This involves throwing a wooden pole high in the air.

You can take a boat trip to Staffa to see amazing rock formations at Fingal's Cave.

Scotland's rivers and lochs are full of salmon and there are many salmon farms along the west coast.

The Trossachs is a lovely area of mountains, lochs and glens where the daring cattle thief, Rob Roy Macgregor, once lived. You can follow his adventures at the Visitor Centre in Callander, and cruise on Loch Lomond, Britain's largest lake.

COLL

TIREE

STAFFA

MULL

STRATHCLYDE

THE TROSSACHS

Comrie

CENTRAL

Callander

Stirling

Loch Lomond

Bannockburn

JURA

ISLAY

ARRAN

Spooky Slaines Castle inspired Bram Stoker's scary Dracula stories.

Slaines Castle

Aberdeen

GRAMPIAN

Scottish rulers were traditionally crowned at Scone.

TAYSIDE

Scone

Dundee

St Andrews

FIFE

River Spey

Whisky

Scotland is famous for whisky. Lots of it is made in the Spey Valley with barley and soft Highland water.

Aberdeen is the centre of Scotland's important oil industry. Oil is drilled from the seabed below the North Sea.

Marmalade and Dundee fruit cake were first made in Dundee 200 years ago. Jam is made now from local fruit.

Golf was first played at St Andrews 500 years ago. There is a Sea Life Centre here and a Scottish Deer Centre nearby.

Kings and Queens of Scotland

Kenneth MacAlpin became the first king of all Scotland in 843. His family ruled until 1290, after which the English invaded.

King Robert the Bruce beat the English at Bannockburn in 1314. His daughter began the long-ruling Stuart line.

The Stuarts' main home was Stirling Castle. From 1603 to 1714, they also inherited the throne of England and Wales.

27

Northern Scotland

The northern Highlands are one of the most unspoilt areas of Britain, with wild mountains, lochs and moors. They are surrounded by rugged islands, and slashed in two by a deep gorge called the Great Glen which runs from coast to coast. The Orkneys and Shetlands are shown here on the right, although they really lie off the north-east tip of mainland Scotland. Seals and puffins breed on these islands and many ships have been wrecked on their rocky shores.

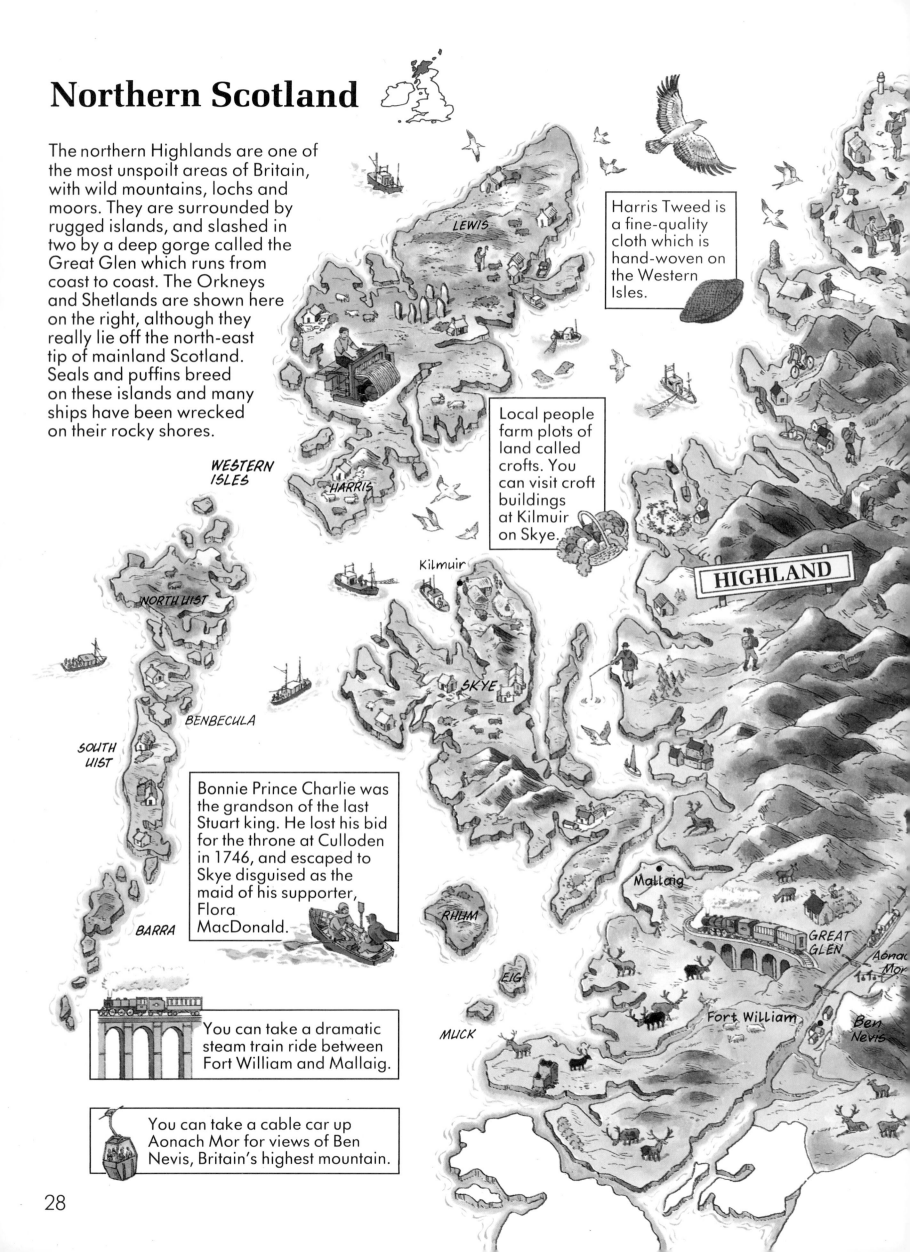

Harris Tweed is a fine-quality cloth which is hand-woven on the Western Isles.

Local people farm plots of land called crofts. You can visit croft buildings at Kilmuir on Skye.

HIGHLAND

LEWIS

WESTERN ISLES

HARRIS

NORTH UIST

Kilmuir

SKYE

BENBECULA

SOUTH UIST

Bonnie Prince Charlie was the grandson of the last Stuart king. He lost his bid for the throne at Culloden in 1746, and escaped to Skye disguised as the maid of his supporter, Flora MacDonald.

BARRA

RHUM

EIG

MUCK

Mallaig

GREAT GLEN

Aonach Mor

Fort William

Ben Nevis

You can take a dramatic steam train ride between Fort William and Mallaig.

You can take a cable car up Aonach Mor for views of Ben Nevis, Britain's highest mountain.

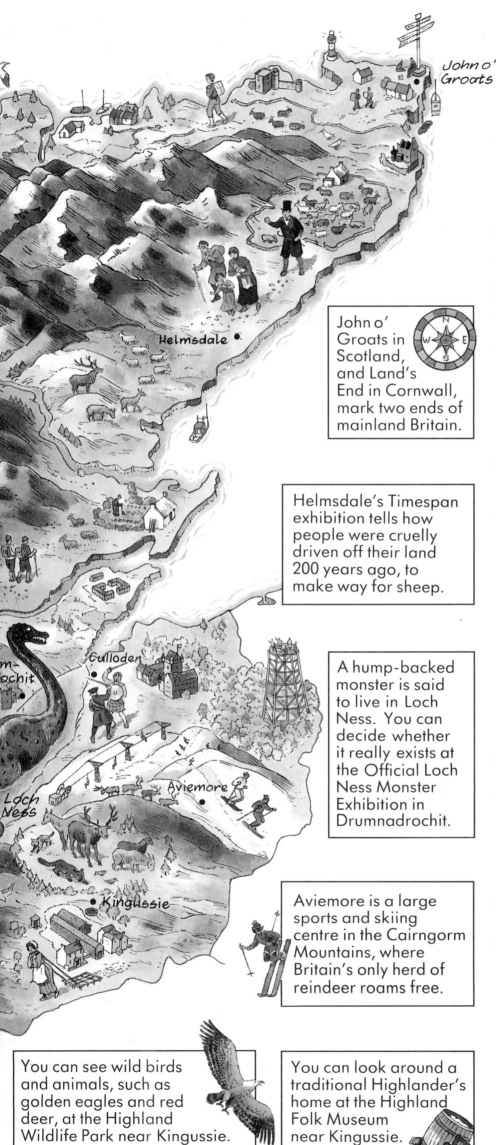

John o' Groats

Helmsdale •

m-
rochit

Culloden

Loch
Ness

Aviemore •

• Kingussie

John o' Groats in Scotland, and Land's End in Cornwall, mark two ends of mainland Britain.

Helmsdale's Timespan exhibition tells how people were cruelly driven off their land 200 years ago, to make way for sheep.

A hump-backed monster is said to live in Loch Ness. You can decide whether it really exists at the Official Loch Ness Monster Exhibition in Drumnadrochit.

Aviemore is a large sports and skiing centre in the Cairngorm Mountains, where Britain's only herd of reindeer roams free.

You can see wild birds and animals, such as golden eagles and red deer, at the Highland Wildlife Park near Kingussie.

You can look around a traditional Highlander's home at the Highland Folk Museum near Kingussie.

The Shetland Islands

Lerwick

FAIR ISLE

Shetland ponies are short and shaggy.

A Viking ship is burned at Lerwick's fire festival in January.

Fair Isle jumpers are named after Fair Isle where they were first knitted.

The Orkney Islands

Skara Brae

Maes Howe

Skara Brae is a neolithic village with stone beds and tables.

You can explore a neolithic tomb at Maes Howe.

29

Northern Ireland

Northern Ireland has mountains, forests, lakes (called loughs) and seaside resorts. It was ruled by England from the Middle Ages but stayed Catholic when England changed to the Protestant religion after 1549. In the 1600s, English and Scottish Protestants were given land to settle here. Their descendants chose to remain under British rule this century when the rest of Ireland became independent. However, many Irish Catholics here wish to join the rest of Ireland. This has led to political and religious conflict between people living here.

Irish sports

Horse-racing and hurling are popular sports in Ireland. Hurling is played a bit like hockey but much faster and with far fewer rules.

St Patrick

Ireland's patron saint, St Patrick, brought Christianity to Ireland in the 5th century. Legend says that he also banished snakes from Ireland.

He built his first church in Armagh and was buried at Downpatrick. People wear the shamrock leaf for St Patrick's Day parades on March 17th.

The Ulster-American Folk Park near Omagh tells how many people left for America during terrible potato famines in the 1840s. The Ulster History Park tells Ireland's earlier history.

History Park

Folk Park

• Omagh

TYRONE

• Ballygawley

Devenish Island

Marble Arch Caves

FERMANAGH

Londonderry

Irish get-togethers

People dance and listen to traditional Irish songs and music in pubs and homes all over Ireland. Many ballads are sung in Gaelic Irish.

Early Christians built a monastery and a look-out tower on Devenish Island.

You can take a boat trip through Marble Arch Caves to see underground lakes.

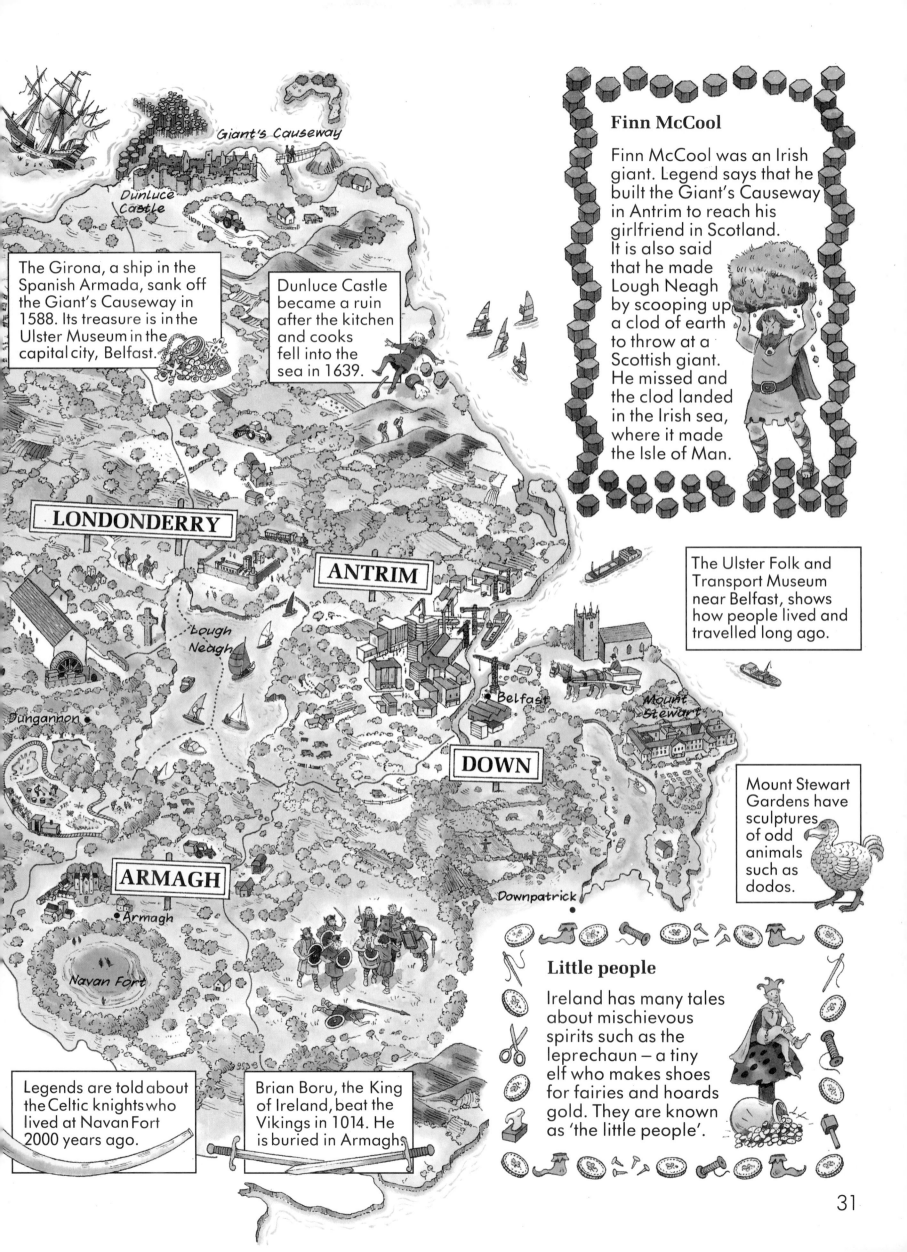

The Girona, a ship in the Spanish Armada, sank off the Giant's Causeway in 1588. Its treasure is in the Ulster Museum in the capital city, Belfast.

Dunluce Castle became a ruin after the kitchen and cooks fell into the sea in 1639.

Giant's Causeway

Dunluce Castle

Finn McCool

Finn McCool was an Irish giant. Legend says that he built the Giant's Causeway in Antrim to reach his girlfriend in Scotland. It is also said that he made Lough Neagh by scooping up a clod of earth to throw at a Scottish giant. He missed and the clod landed in the Irish sea, where it made the Isle of Man.

LONDONDERRY

ANTRIM

Lough Neagh

Dungannon •

The Ulster Folk and Transport Museum near Belfast, shows how people lived and travelled long ago.

• Belfast

Mount Stewart

DOWN

Mount Stewart Gardens have sculptures of odd animals such as dodos.

ARMAGH

• Armagh

Navan Fort

Downpatrick •

Little people

Ireland has many tales about mischievous spirits such as the leprechaun – a tiny elf who makes shoes for fairies and hoards gold. They are known as 'the little people'.

Legends are told about the Celtic knights who lived at Navan Fort 2000 years ago.

Brian Boru, the King of Ireland, beat the Vikings in 1014. He is buried in Armagh.

Index

Alton Towers, 17
Anglesey, 22
Antrim, 31
Armagh, 31
Avon,12

bagpipes, 24, 25, 26
Battle of Hastings, 4, 11
Beamish Museum, 20
Beatles, 19
Beaulieu Museum, 10
Bedfordshire, 13
Bedruthan, 8
Belfast, 31
Ben Nevis, 28
Berkshire, 12–13
Big Ben, 6
Bluebell Railway, 11
Bonnie Prince Charlie, 28
Borders, 25
Boudicca, 15
Brian Boru, 31
British Museum, 7,14
Brontës, The, 21
Brown, Capability, 13
Brunel, I. K, 12
Buckingham Palace, 6
Buckinghamshire, 13
Burns, Robert, 24

Cambridgeshire, 15
canals, 19,
Cardiff, 23
Caernarfon Castle, 22
Central region, 26–27
Channel Islands, 3, 10
Channel Tunnel, 11
Cheddar Gorge, 9
Cheshire, 19
cider, 9
Civil War, 4, 17
Cleveland, 20–21
Clwyd, 22
Constable, John, 15
Cornwall, 8
Cotswolds, 12
cream teas, 9
cricket, 10
Cromwell, Oliver 4, 17
Cumbria, 18
Cutty Sark, 7

Dartmoor, 9
Derbyshire, 17
Devon, 9
Dorset, 10
Down, 31
Drake, Francis, 9
Dumfries and Galloway,
    24–25
Durham, 20–21
Dyfed, 23

Edinburgh, 25
Eisteddfod, 22
England, 2, 6–21
Essex, 15
European Community, 3

Fens, The, 14
Fermanagh, 30
Fife, 27
Forth Rail Bridge, 25

Giant's Causeway, 31
Glamorgan, 23
Gloucestershire, 12
Government, 3,
Grampian, 27
Greater Manchester, 19
Great Glen, 28–29
Gulf Stream, 2, 8
Gwent, 23
Gwynedd, 22–23

Hadrian's Wall, 20
haggis, 24
Hampshire, 10
Harrods, 6
Heathrow, 11
Hereford and Worcester,
    16–17
Hertfordshire, 13
Highland Games, 26
Highland region, 28–29
Humberside, 20
hurling, 30

Industrial Revolution, 4, 16
Ironbridge Museums, 16
Isle of Man, 3, 18, 31
Isle of Wight, 10
Isles of Scilly, 8

John o'Groats, 29
Jorvick Centre, 21

Kent, 11
Kew Gardens, 7
King Aurthur, 9

Lake District, 18
Lancashire, 19
Land's End, 8
language, 2, 22, 30
Leicestershire, 17
leprechaun, 31
Lincolnshire, 14
Loch Ness Monster, 29
London, 2, 6–7
Londonderry, 30–31
Lothian, 25

MacCool, Finn, 31
MacGregor, Rob Roy, 26
Madame Tussaud's 6
marmalade, 27
Mary Rose, 10
Merseyside, 19
morris dancers, 15

New Forest, 20
Newton, Isaac, 14
Norfolk, 15
Northamptonshire, 17
Northern Ireland, 2, 30–31
Northumberland, 20
North York Moors, 21
Nottinghamshire, 17

oil, 3, 27
Orkney Islands, 28, 29
Oxfordshire, 12–13

Peak District, 17
Pennine Hills, 20–21
Potter, Beatrix, 18
Powys, 22–23
Punch and Judy, 11

Robert the Bruce, 25, 27
Robin Hood, 17
Royal Family, 3, 6
Royal Pavilion, 11
rugby, 23

Scotland, 2, 24–29
Shakespeare, William, 17
Sherwood Forest, 17
Shetland Islands, 28, 29
Shropshire, 16
Skye, 28
smugglers, 8
Snowdon, 22
Somerset, 9
Staffordshire, 16–17
Stephenson, George, 20
Stonehenge, 12
St Patrick, 30
St Paul's Cathedral, 7
Strathclyde, 24, 26
Suffolk, 15
Surrey, 10–11
Sussex, 10–11

tartan, 26
Tayside, 26–27
Thames River, 7, 12, 13
thatched roofs, 14
Trossachs, The, 26
Turpin, Dick, 15
Tyne and Wear, 20
Tyrone, 30–31

Ultimate, The, 21
Union Jack, 2
United Kingdom, 2–3, 6

Wales 2, 22–23
Wars of the Roses, 5, 17
Warwick Castle, 17
Warwickshire, 17
Wedgwood china, 16
Western Isles, 28
West Midlands, 16–17
Westminster Abbey, 6
Whipsnade Zoo, 12, 13
whisky, 27
William the Conqueror,
    4, 11
Wiltshire, 12
Windsor Castle, 13
Wookey Hole, 9
Wordsworth, William, 18

Yorkshire, 21
Yorkshire pudding, 21

First published 1992 by Usborne Publishing Ltd, Usborne House, 83–85 Saffron Hill, London EC1N 8RT.

Copyright © Usborne Publishing Ltd, 1992. The name Usborne and the device 🎈 are Trade Marks of Usborne Publishing Ltd.